Queen ELIZABETH I

Queen
ELIZABETH I

Kate Havelin

Lerner Publications Company
Minneapolis

To Elizabeth. History is incomplete without her story.
And to my family, who understand that history matters
more than clean laundry.

A&E and **BIOGRAPHY** are trademarks of the A&E Television
Networks, registered in the United States and other countries.

Some of the people profiled in this series have also been featured in the
acclaimed BIOGRAPHY® series, on A&E Network, which is available on
videocassette from A&E Home Video.

Lerner Publications Company
A division of Lerner Publishing Group
241 First Avenue North
Minneapolis, MN 55401 U.S.A.

Website address: www.lernerbooks.com

Library of Congress Cataloging-in-Publication Data

Havelin, Kate 1961–
    Queen Elizabeth I / by Kate Havelin.
      p.   cm. — (A&E biography)
    Includes bibliographical references and index.
    ISBN: 0–8225–0029–9 (lib. bdg. : alk. paper)
    1. Elizabeth I, Queen of England, 1533–1603—Juvenile literature.
    2. Great Britain—History—Elizabeth, 1558–1603—Juvenile literature.
    3. Queens—Great Britain——Biography—Juvenile literature.
    [1. Elizabeth I, Queen of England, 1533–1603.   2. Kings, queens, rulers,
    etc.   3. Women—Biography.   4. Great Britain—History—Elizabeth,
    1558–1603.]   I. Title.   II. Biography (Lerner Publications Company)
    DA355.H38 2002
    942.05'5'092–dc21
    [B]   2001002221

Manufactured in the United States of America
1 2 3 4 5 6 – JR – 07 06 05 04 03 02

CONTENTS

This portrait, which hangs in Windsor Castle in England, shows Elizabeth in her early teens. The book in her hands and the one behind her show her interest in learning.

Chapter **ONE**

YOUNG ELIZABETH

TWENTY-YEAR-OLD **E**LIZABETH **LISTENED TO MEN SHE** had known all her life tell her they had orders to imprison her in the Tower of London. The orders came from Elizabeth's half sister, Mary Tudor, queen of England. The queen wanted to shut her sister away in the Tower. The Tower was where Elizabeth's mother, Anne Boleyn, had been locked up before being beheaded. The Tower was where countless criminals and political victims spent their last days.

Elizabeth was accused of being a traitor who plotted to kill her sister, the queen. A nobleman named Sir Thomas Wyatt had organized a rebellion to kill Mary and then crown Elizabeth. Elizabeth swore she knew nothing of Wyatt's rebellion. Her only hope to avoid imprisonment was to appeal directly to her older sister. Elizabeth begged the courtiers who came to take her to the Tower to let her see Mary. They refused. She pleaded with them to let her write a letter. The courtiers agreed to this request and fetched her ink, pen, and paper.

Elizabeth began writing a letter she hoped would save her life. Her fear runs through the letter in awkward phrases and omitted words. Her normally elegant handwriting is scrawled. Slowly, she filled one whole page and part of a second sheet. When she finished writing, she slashed long lines through the rest of the page. She did not want anyone to add anything to her letter that would anger Mary.

In her letter, Elizabeth begged for mercy: "I humbly crave to speak with your Highness . . . I humbly crave but only one word of answer from yourself."

Mary never answered, and the next morning, Palm Sunday, March 17, 1554, the courtiers came once again to take Elizabeth to the Tower. In a bitter cold rain, they traveled by boat along the Thames River and entered the massive stone and brick fortress.

Stepping out of the boat, Elizabeth sat down on the damp stone steps leading into the Tower and refused to go on. "Oh Lord!" she cried, "I never thought to come here as a prisoner!" The courtiers escorting Elizabeth finally persuaded her to rise. She walked on toward the cold and drafty rooms—her new home.

Elizabeth was allowed to keep a few of her favorite

Hundreds of people were executed at the Tower of London, center, with four towers, *including Anne Boleyn, Katherine Howard, and Lady Jane Grey. For two months, Elizabeth herself was held prisoner there, not knowing whether she would share the same fate.*

ladies and servants with her. She stayed in the Queen's Rooms, a corner section of the Tower where her mother had stayed before her execution. To while away the tedious hours, Elizabeth, the Tower's most famous prisoner, was allowed to walk along the brick and stone battlements. She also did needlepoint and embroidered a book cover with a Latin phrase that translates, "Tenacious virtue overcomes all—Elizabeth the Prisoner."

Each morning the princess awoke not knowing if she would live. Royal prisoners sentenced to death were usually beheaded. Elizabeth didn't want an executioner to cut off her head with an ax. Axes were used for executing commoners. She requested a sword from France, just like the kind used to behead her mother.

Finally, on the anniversary of her mother's execution, May 19, 1554, Elizabeth was told to leave her rooms. She thought she was being led to her death. Instead, she was leaving the Tower. Her sister, the queen, had released her. Elizabeth was not free; she would still be under house arrest. But she had survived the Tower.

All her life, Elizabeth never forgot being locked in the Tower of London. Years later, she still thanked God "for pulling me from the prison to the palace."

"BOYS WILL FOLLOW"

Elizabeth's story began before she was born. It started with her father, King Henry VIII of the house of Tudor, who was desperate for a son. By 1525 King Henry had been married for sixteen years to Catherine of Aragon, yet they had only one child who survived infancy. Princess Mary was born in 1516, but Henry, like most English people, believed women were not able to lead a country. He wanted a son to follow him as king and feared Catherine would never produce a healthy boy.

Henry VIII lived to be fifty-six and had six wives and three children. Elizabeth was his middle child.

Henry found a woman he wanted to be his new wife, if he could get rid of Catherine. Most people in Europe were Catholic, and divorce was against church law. Since the pope, the head of the Catholic Church, refused to annul the marriage (to declare it was never legal), the king decided to form his own Church of England. It took years for Henry to establish the English church, but in 1533 Henry annulled his marriage to Queen Catherine and married a young woman with flashing black eyes named Anne Boleyn.

Anne Boleyn was married to Henry VIII from 1533, when she was pregnant with Elizabeth, until 1536, when she was beheaded on the grounds of infidelity.

By the time Henry and Anne were officially married in May 1533, Anne was six months pregnant. The physicians and fortune-tellers assured the king the baby was a boy. Henry couldn't decide whether to name his heir-to-be Edward or Henry, and court scribes had already written the formal letters announcing the birth of a prince.

Then, on September 7, 1533, Anne Boleyn gave birth to a girl. Scribes quickly changed the letters. Henry canceled the joust scheduled to celebrate the baby's birth. The king cursed the midwives and physicians at the birth and told Anne simply, "By God's grace, boys will follow." The king was too disappointed to attend his daughter's christening, but he named the baby in honor of his beautiful, intelligent mother: Elizabeth.

A LOVED—AND HATED—PRINCESS

Baby Elizabeth was treated like the princess she was. She had two cradles—one decorated in crimson silk and covered with a fur blanket, the other made of carved wood painted gold. Anne Boleyn gave her daughter clothes made of damask and satin, and caps embroidered with gold.

Many people hated Anne Boleyn and her baby. Most Europeans did not approve of divorce. People in Spain, Catherine's home, were outraged at the way Henry had pushed her aside. Even many English people called Anne Boleyn the Great Whore and baby Elizabeth the Little Whore. They blamed Anne for wrecking Henry and Catherine's marriage. Henry had ordered the heralds who announced Elizabeth's birth also to announce that Catherine's daughter, seventeen-year-old Mary, was no longer a princess. She could not succeed Henry to the throne. Princess Elizabeth could become queen if Henry died, but Henry still wanted a son.

Henry soon grew tired of Anne, and after Catherine died, Henry felt he could dispose of his second wife as well. Anne was charged with treason and adultery. She was accused of having had love affairs with other men and having plotted to kill Henry. She was sentenced to death, and on May 19, 1536, Anne Boleyn was beheaded.

Elizabeth was two years and eight months old when her mother was executed. Hundreds, perhaps thousands, of people watched the royal beheading, but Elizabeth was miles away. As was the custom in royal families, she had been living with her own household of servants for most of her young life. Still, the toddler soon realized her world had changed dramatically.

When Anne Boleyn was beheaded, Elizabeth lost her title. She was no longer in line to succeed the king. Henry had annulled his marriage to Anne, saying an earlier love affair he had had with Anne's sister invalidated their legal marriage. That meant Elizabeth was no longer a legal heir. Henry declared her a bastard—a child born outside of marriage. But Elizabeth still was the king's daughter. More than two dozen servants

cared for her. Henry wanted his daughter to be sur-
rounded by "ancient and sad persons" to make sure
she would grow up serious. He did not want her to be
spirited and joyful like her mother.

ANOTHER WIFE FOR HENRY

Within days of Anne's death, Henry married for the
third time. This wife, Jane Seymour, soon gave Henry
the son he desired. But Jane died within two weeks of
giving birth to a prince, Edward, in 1537. Edward was
Henry's hope for the future. Elizabeth was all but for-
gotten, staying mostly at Hatfield, her royal home,
twenty miles north of London. Like other upper-class
and royal girls, Elizabeth spent many hours practicing
needlework. By the time she was six, she had already
stitched her two-year-old brother a shirt. She likely
had learned to read and write by that age as well and
was just beginning to study Latin.

While Elizabeth studied and sewed, Henry was ready
for the altar again. He married his fourth wife, Anne
of Cleves, in 1540. She was a foreign princess and
didn't please the aging king, so that same year he
annulled the marriage and wedded yet again. Henry's
fifth wife, Katherine Howard, was a cousin of Anne
Boleyn. Less than two years later, Henry had this
young wife beheaded, too. Elizabeth was eight years
old when Katherine Howard died in 1542. Later that
year, Elizabeth told her friend Robert Dudley that she
would never marry. No one knows how she felt about

her father's many marriages, but chances are they sent a strong message about how dangerous marriage could be for a woman.

In 1543 Henry married a wealthy widow named Katherine Parr. She was his sixth wife, and his fourth wife in seven years. Henry was getting old and sick. His leg was infected, his body grossly overweight. Katherine Parr would take care of him. The king's sixth wife was kind to all three surviving Tudor children. Mary, Elizabeth, and Edward even traveled with Henry and his new wife right after their wedding. Queen Katherine oversaw the education of the younger two royal children. She had some of the

Katherine Parr married Henry VIII in 1543. She was Henry's last wife and managed to outlive him.

country's brightest scholars tutor Elizabeth and Edward. Brother and sister studied Latin, Greek, French, and Italian. They also learned history, math, geography, and astronomy. History was one of Elizabeth's favorite subjects. All her life, she would continue to read and study and learn. Along with intellectual pursuits, the royal children also spent time learning to ride horses and play music. Elizabeth played the virginals, a keyboard instrument. She also practiced sewing and dancing.

It was a busy, productive time for Elizabeth. She loved learning, studying languages, and translating historic works. But before she turned thirteen, her peaceful life of studying with Edward would change again.

Edward VI, the long awaited male heir, took the throne upon Henry's death. He was nine years old.

Chapter **TWO**

THE KING
IS DEAD!

EARLY IN THE MORNING OF JANUARY 28, 1547,
King Henry VIII died. But instead of announcing the
death immediately, his advisors kept it a secret for
three days. They were plotting how they would control
the throne.

One councillor, Edward Seymour, Jane's brother,
went to Hertford Castle to get his nephew, nine-year-
old Prince Edward. Seymour took Edward to another
royal home, Enfield, where Elizabeth was. Once the
young brother and sister were together, Seymour told
them their father was dead. They were orphans, but
as royalty, they would never lack for people who
wanted to help them—or control them.

By February 20, 1547, Edward had been crowned

king. His uncle, Edward Seymour, was named Lord Protector, the young king's chief advisor.

Edward's coronation sent the first strong signals that England had changed. Advisors dramatically shortened the lengthy traditional ceremony. They gave the new king more power, indicating that he was chosen by God to be king. They intended Edward, not the Catholic pope, to rule his country's souls. Edward and his advisors began a series of anti-Catholic reforms, strengthening the Church of England his father had founded.

"SWEET SISTER TEMPERANCE"

Elizabeth was raised as a Protestant. She was comfortable with the Church of England. But her older sister, Mary, was a fervent Catholic whose religion offended Edward. Elizabeth had grown up studying with Edward, was close to his age, and was on good terms with her brother. Edward called Elizabeth Sweet Sister Temperance, a nickname honoring her moderate approach to religion and life. Edward had had little contact with his much older sister, Mary.

Elizabeth and Edward had exchanged portraits. Hers, painted when she was thirteen, shows a slender and serious girl with pale skin and dark eyes, dressed in rich red brocade, her long and graceful hands clasping a book, while another book sits open by her side. Elizabeth continued her studies, mastering Latin and Greek, French and Italian. A letter to Edward sent along with the portrait shows the pride the princess had in her intelligence. Elizabeth wrote, "For the face I grant I might well blush to offer, but for the mind I shall never be ashamed."

It's likely Elizabeth knew that many people still hated her. They blamed her mother for Henry's divorce and the rise of the Church of England. Henry's will put Mary and Elizabeth in line for the throne, but it didn't make them legitimate. In the eyes of the law and the world, Elizabeth was still a bastard—since Henry had declared that his marriage to Anne was invalid and had not been sanctioned by the Church of England. It was a bitter birthright that no doubt shaped Elizabeth's spirit. She learned to hide her feelings and keep her heart to herself.

She seemed to be a sober person who, like her tutors, disdained dancing, gambling, and music in favor of more serious pursuits. She dressed plainly, often in black velvet. She didn't wear jewels or fancy crowns. Instead of fixing her hair in elaborate styles, Elizabeth simply kept her golden red hair straight.

Elizabeth certainly could afford fancy clothes and jewels. Henry willed her and Mary each three thousand pounds a year. (A commoner might earn two pounds a year.) The sisters were also promised ten thousand pounds dowry, assuming the Royal Council approved their marriages. And the royal princesses received homes and property—but only until they married. Then, the royal property went back to the crown.

After Henry's death, Elizabeth moved in with her

stepmother, Katherine Parr, to finish her education. Jane Grey, another Seymour relative, joined the household as well. It was common for a great lady to oversee teenaged girls. Katherine was a good mother to Elizabeth. She valued religion and learning. At age thirty-five, Katherine had already outlived two elderly husbands. Now, she was ready to marry for love. Within months of Henry's death, Katherine wedded Thomas Seymour, the Lord Protector's brother. She loved Thomas, but he mostly loved power.

A Brush with Danger

Thomas Seymour was jealous of the status of his older brother, Edward Seymour. He wasn't satisfied that his brother had named him Lord Admiral. He wanted to be the power behind the throne, too. Some believe he only married Katherine Parr to get close to Elizabeth, who was second in line for the crown after her older sister, Mary. At least ten women of the Tudor family were in the succession. After Mary and Elizabeth came the children and grandchildren of Henry's sisters.

Thomas Seymour supposedly had tried to marry Elizabeth but failed to get the Royal Council's approval. Yet marriage to Katherine allowed Seymour to see Elizabeth daily. The high-spirited Seymour quickly began flirting with the fourteen-year-old princess. He was thirty-eight, handsome, and a man of the world. Early in the morning, Seymour would go into

Elizabeth's bedchamber and shout a hearty good morning before she was fully dressed. It was said sometimes he would "strike her upon the back or on the buttocks familiarly."

Elizabeth's lady-in-waiting, Kat Ashley, tried to discourage Seymour's early morning visits, saying they were causing scandal. Seymour protested it was innocent fun. He began coming to Elizabeth's room in the morning with Katherine, who was by this time pregnant. The

By marrying widow Katherine Parr, Thomas Seymour was able to position himself closer to Elizabeth.

couple would tickle Elizabeth while she was still in bed. Some books say there was a love triangle—both Katherine and Elizabeth in love with Seymour. Others say Elizabeth was the victim of sexual harassment. It's rumored that one day Katherine found Elizabeth in Seymour's arms. What is known is that Elizabeth soon left Katherine's home.

Elizabeth went to stay with another noble family. She and Katherine exchanged friendly letters, with Elizabeth apologizing for anything she might have done to upset her loving stepmother. Elizabeth continued her studies but suffered headaches, colds, and other complaints. She may have felt guilty that she was not there to be with Katherine, who was close to giving birth, and she was not there when Katherine died, along with her baby, in childbirth. Two days after her beloved stepmother died, Elizabeth turned fifteen. The young princess continued to suffer what were likely stress-induced illnesses throughout her teenage years.

Thomas Seymour, now a widower, once again tried to woo Elizabeth. He talked to Thomas Parry, who oversaw Elizabeth's money, to find out how much Lady Elizabeth was worth. At the same time, Seymour was plotting to displace his brother, the Lord Protector, and win King Edward's attention. In January 1549, Thomas Seymour sneaked into the young king's chamber, but was caught after he shot a dog that had started barking. It's not clear that Thomas Seymour was trying to overthrow the king, but he was found guilty of treason.

Elizabeth's closest servants, Kat Ashley and Thomas Parry, were taken to the Tower and questioned about Elizabeth's role in Thomas Seymour's schemes. They protested she was innocent. Elizabeth herself was harshly questioned for weeks. She and her servants swore they were not part of Seymour's plot. Elizabeth and her servants avoided punishment, but Thomas Seymour was executed on March 20, 1549.

For months afterward, Elizabeth maintained a low profile. She was not welcome at court. She learned once again to guard her feelings. Meanwhile, plots continued to swirl behind the throne. Thomas Seymour wasn't the only Englishman who had wanted to be the young king's most powerful advisor. By fall 1549, another nobleman, John Dudley, father of Elizabeth's childhood friend Robert, had overthrown the Lord Protector.

With John Dudley in control, the king's councillors put forth a new Book of Common Prayer in English, not Latin. In the past, prayer books were only printed in Latin, the language of the Catholic Church. Printing prayer books in English allowed people who didn't read Latin to pray for themselves. It was another dramatic step in reforming the church.

In May 1553, John Dudley convinced another son, Guildford Dudley, to marry Jane Grey. She was among the many Tudor women in line for the throne. King

Edward's health was worsening, and it seemed clear that someone else would soon rule England. Edward had never been strong. He was born with syphilis, inherited from his parents. By this time, he also had tuberculosis, a disease of the lungs. The question on everyone's mind was who next would wear the crown?

Influenced by John Dudley, Edward decided that neither of his sisters should become queen. After all, their father had annulled his marriages to Mary's and Elizabeth's mothers and declared the girls were bastards. So Edward instead named his cousin Jane Grey and her future sons as his successors. It's more likely Edward changed the succession because he didn't want his Catholic sister, Mary, to become queen and destroy the Protestant Church of England.

On July 6, 1553, Edward, only fifteen, died. Lady Jane Grey was named queen, but she would not rule long. Within days, forces loyal to Mary and the rightful Tudor succession overthrew Queen Jane. On July 19, 1553, Mary was proclaimed queen.

A CATHOLIC QUEEN

Mary was thirty-seven years old but seemed older. She had endured years of sickness and unhappiness. She had grown up seeing her mother cast aside, her religion challenged, and her younger half sister and brother rise in power.

Elizabeth supported Mary's right to the throne. The nineteen-year-old Elizabeth rode into London with an

Mary Tudor, or Mary I, tried to restore Catholicism as the state religion. She ordered the execution of hundreds of Protestants, for which she earned the nickname Bloody Mary.

army of one thousand horsemen, a clear sign she would use her power to help Mary. At first, the sisters got along well. But the difference in religion quickly created a strain.

Queen Mary encouraged churches in London to return to the Catholic Mass, which a few churches did. Yet most Londoners were Protestants. Very few English people under the age of thirty-five were Catholic. Protests broke out. The religious tension grew worse when Mary chose to marry a Catholic, King Philip II of Spain.

Under pressure from her sister, Elizabeth converted to Catholicism. But still Elizabeth was made to feel uncomfortable at Mary's Catholic court. Mary couldn't forget how her mother, Catherine of Aragon, had been displaced by Anne Boleyn. Anne's daughter, Elizabeth, would never become queen if Mary could help it.

DANGER, AGAIN

By December 1553, Elizabeth had left Mary's court. One month later, on January 25, 1554, Sir Thomas Wyatt began a rebellion to force Mary from the throne and replace her with Protestant Elizabeth. Wyatt's rebellion failed within three weeks. He was arrested on February 7, 1554. The question was, would Elizabeth suffer as well?

Once again Elizabeth insisted she was innocent, just as she had after Thomas Seymour was arrested. She claimed she knew nothing of Wyatt's plot. Mary demanded Elizabeth come to court, but the princess was sick. She begged for time to recover before returning to London. Mary sent her physicians and ordered Elizabeth to return to London. Elizabeth was suffering from migraines. Her body was swollen by a kidney ailment that would continue to affect her frequently during Mary's stressful reign.

Elizabeth had reason to be sick and afraid. After the brief uprising, Mary and her councillors were determined to rid England of Protestant protest. On February 12, the executioner beheaded Lady Jane Grey, the seventeen-year-old who had been queen for less than two weeks.

Thomas Wyatt, a Protestant supporter of Elizabeth, led a rebellion against Queen Mary I.

WHO WAS WHO IN EUROPE

When the Tudor family was ruling England, the great powers of Europe were Spain, France, and the Holy Roman Empire. Maps of the period show a political landscape dramatically different from modern Europe, made up of many small city-states and a few dynasties that controlled most of the land and power. One great power, the Holy Roman Empire, was a vast collection of city-states such as Bavaria, Saxony, and Westphalia. The Empire stretched east from France through much of modern Germany to the western border of Poland and extended as far south as modern Italy and as far north as Denmark. Archduke Charles V ruled the Holy Roman Empire from 1520 until he abdicated in 1555. Charles also had inherited Spain from his grandfather Ferdinand in 1516, but Charles spent most of his energy on the Holy Roman Empire dealing with countless political and religious intrigues.

Charles's son Philip II ruled Spain for much of the time Henry VIII's children were in power. Philip also controlled Portugal and the Low Countries, which were composed of the Netherlands and Belgium, as well as other small city-states. He was the great-grandson of Ferdinand and Isabella, earlier rulers of Spain, who were also the grandparents of Mary Tudor. So later, when Philip and Mary married, the two strands of Spain's powerful lineage were reunited.

That same day, finally obeying Mary's orders, Elizabeth began a slow, painful journey back to London. Eleven days later, she reached London, opening the curtains of her litter so people could see she was

France was under the control of the House of Valois. Francis I ruled his country with as much charisma as Henry VIII ruled England. When Francis I died, his son Henry II became king. When Henry II died unexpectedly, his son Francis II became king. The power behind the throne rested with Francis's mother-in-law, Mary of Guise, whose daughter Mary, Queen of Scots was married to the new French king. When Francis II also died young, his mother, Catherine de Médicis, took control. She had borne ten children and ended up serving as regent (ruling power) for two of her young sons, Charles IX and Henry III.

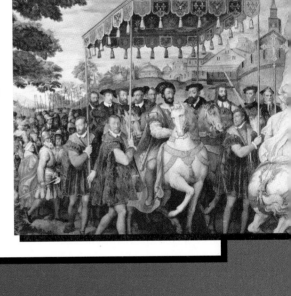

Charles V, the Holy Roman emperor, and Francis I, king of France, head a procession entering Paris.

indeed ill. Clad in white, her face pale, young Elizabeth came back to a hostile queen. Bloodied heads of traitors lined the poles of London Bridge. The day Elizabeth reached Whitehall in London, Lady

Jane Grey's father, the duke of Suffolk, was killed.

Mary's councillors wanted to prove Elizabeth was part of a plot to overthrow the queen. During his trial on March 15, Thomas Wyatt continued to deny Elizabeth's knowledge of the plot. Still, the next day Mary ordered Elizabeth to be taken to the Tower. Wyatt was executed on April 11, 1554, after again proclaiming Elizabeth's innocence. Elizabeth remained in the Tower's circular Queen's Rooms. She asked if the scaffold used to behead Jane Grey had been removed. It remained standing, across the Tower courtyard. Elizabeth waited.

The country was on edge. Mary realized civil war might erupt if she killed her popular Protestant sister. So she released Elizabeth from prison in the Tower. Instead, she was to be under house arrest at Woodstock, a palace in northern England, a Catholic stronghold.

Elizabeth knew she was not out of danger and feared she would still be killed by Mary. Her first day out of the Tower, she told her gentleman usher, "For this night, I think to die." It was an uncertain time for the twenty-year-old, who was felt to be a threat to the queen. Along the roads to Woodstock, though, countless people watched her pass, welcoming her with the cry, "God save Your Grace!" Women prepared special cakes and gifts. Elizabeth was overwhelmed and finally had to ask villagers to stop giving her presents.

At Woodstock, Elizabeth was given four rooms in

the gatehouse, not the royal apartment. She was allowed to walk in the orchards, but she was not free to write or speak with friends. Mary chose Elizabeth's ladies-in-waiting. Anyone who seemed too friendly to the prisoner princess was dismissed. Elizabeth said that under Mary's reign, she learned to be silent. The young princess learned not to confide in people, but she did reveal a bit of herself in a poem. Etched with a diamond on one of Woodstock's windows, the couplet reads, "Much suspected of me/ Nothing proved can be/ Quoth Elizabeth prisoner."

Elizabeth remained a prisoner at Woodstock for

During the reign of Queen Mary, prisoners were beheaded at the Tower of London on a block and with an axe like these. The heads were stuck on poles on London Bridge.

almost a year. In July 1554, Mary married Philip II of Spain. The court was tense with angry disputes between English courtiers and Philip's Spanish servants. Mary grew increasingly militant about abolishing her father's Church of England, which she hated. More than two hundred and fifty Protestants were burned at the stake. The queen earned the nickname Bloody Mary. Many English people looked upon Elizabeth as their last hope. One poet wrote, "When these with violence were burned to death/ We wished for our Elizabeth."

Mary's reign was probably Elizabeth's darkest time. She and many others feared for their lives. Although she was the second richest landowner in the country, Elizabeth was penniless because she did not have control of her property while under house arrest. Robert Dudley, her childhood friend, sold some of his land to help the impoverished princess.

The future seemed grim. Philip persuaded his queen to free Elizabeth. Mary was sickly, and some say he realized that she might die. If that happened, Philip could marry Elizabeth. Mary wanted her younger sister to marry Philip's cousin, Philibert of Savoy. Elizabeth refused. Even when Mary threatened to send her sister back to the Tower, Elizabeth remained firm. She wrote Mary, "The afflictions suffered by me are such that they have ridded me of any desire for a husband. . . . I would rather die."

Elizabeth would say later that by 1558 she felt she was being buried alive. But the bitter and bloody reign of Mary was ending. On November 7, 1558, as she lay dying, Mary recognized Elizabeth as her successor. She only asked that Elizabeth maintain the Catholic religion. A week later, on November 17, the forty-two-year-old queen died.

Legend has it that Elizabeth was at her residence, Hatfield, reading the Bible in Greek by an oak tree, when a horseman arrived, bearing the royal ring and the news of Mary's death. The twenty-five-year-old Elizabeth would be queen. She fell to her knees, crying, "Time has brought us to this place. This is the Lord's doing, and it is marvelous in our eyes."

This painting is commonly known as the Coronation Portrait. Elizabeth holds a scepter in her right hand as a symbol of justice and power. The orb in her left hand symbolizes the ruler's hand upon the world.

Chapter **THREE**

ELIZABETH IS CROWNED

SIX HOURS AFTER MARY'S DEATH, ELIZABETH WAS proclaimed queen. It was the smoothest transition of power England had enjoyed in more than a century. The bastard princess, whose mother had been beheaded, and who herself had gone to the Tower in disgrace, would now wear the crown.

Elizabeth moved quickly to show the people that her reign would not be like her sister's. One of her first acts was to name William Cecil as her chief secretary of state. At age thirty-eight, Cecil was her youngest advisor and the one she would listen to most. When she swore Cecil into her Privy Council (cabinet), the new queen said she expected straight talk from him. "This judgement I have of you," Elizabeth told Cecil,

William Cecil served on Elizabeth's Privy Council from 1558, when Elizabeth was crowned, until his death in 1598.

"that you will not be corrupted with any manner of gift, and that you will be faithful to the State, and that without respect of my private will you will give me that counsel that you think best." For his loyalty and strong will, Elizabeth nicknamed Cecil Sir Spirit.

It was Cecil who drew up Elizabeth's accession proclamation, her first official document. It told England of Mary's death and affirmed that the country would now be bound to Elizabeth. Protestants expected they would gain control and be able to punish Catholics as Bloody Mary had punished them. But Elizabeth clearly wanted to avoid further religious strife. When she signed her first documents and listed her titles, Elizabeth simply wrote "&c,." meaning "and so forth" rather than add "Supreme Head of the Church of England." She knew many people believed a woman could not lead the church and didn't want to offend them. But Elizabeth made it clear she would be head of her government. She promptly removed more than two dozen of Mary's Catholic councillors and named just ten of her own. That slimmed down the unwieldy Privy Council to a more manageable size. Elizabeth would listen to her advisors—and rule as she saw best.

By Christmas 1558, the new queen was sending signals about her views on that most divisive subject—religion. On Christmas Day, Elizabeth went to hear Mass in the Royal Chapel. She scolded the priest for using Catholic ritual and walked out when he defied her. Two days later, Elizabeth proclaimed that clerics should use English for the Gospel reading and use the litany in English, written by Thomas Cranmer, the archbishop whom Mary had had burned at the stake.

CORONATION

On January 14, 1559, bells pealed and bonfires blazed throughout London. Elizabeth was in the Tower again, but this time she had reason to celebrate. It was traditional that royalty stay in the Tower for a few days before their coronation. Elizabeth's ceremony would blend old and new.

For the most ornate day of her life, Elizabeth chose to wear a hand-me-down. Dressed in her sister's elaborate gold and silver coronation gown, Elizabeth made her way through the streets of London riding atop a large litter (an enclosed couch, carried by attendants) trimmed in gold and satin with room for gifts from loyal subjects. An old woman gave her a sprig of rosemary, which Elizabeth held tight. A young girl presented a Bible in English, which Elizabeth kissed, to the crowd's delight. Over streets freshly graveled, past houses newly painted, the royal procession glided from the Tower to Westminster Abbey, where Elizabeth would be crowned.

The imperial state crown is worn by the English monarch at coronation and all state occasions. This current crown contains gems taken from the earrings of Queen Elizabeth I.

This illustration of Elizabeth's coronation procession shows her riding in a coach pulled by horses, although she actually rode atop a litter, carried by attendants.

The procession and pageants were glorious. But finding a bishop to crown Elizabeth had been difficult. The leading churchmen were Catholic, like Mary. Even the moderates had been offended by Elizabeth's Christmas Day exit from Mass. In the end, a junior bishop named Owen Oglethorpe oversaw the coronation. The new queen was anointed with holy oil and presented with the crown and scepter of gold, but Oglethorpe read the Gospel in English as well as Latin. Elizabeth would be queen on her own terms.

Despite the glory of her coronation, Queen Elizabeth's start seemed bleak. One account described the situation: "The Queen poor, the realm exhausted, the nobility poor and decayed. Want of good captains and soldiers. The people out of order."

MONEY PROBLEMS

It seems hard to believe that a queen who received three hundred thousand pounds annually could be poor when the servant of a courtier might earn fifty pounds a year. But Elizabeth's income had to cover all the costs of her government. She paid for the food and salaries of everyone at court, which took some forty thousand pounds a year. She paid for her coronation, which totaled almost seventeen thousand pounds. She inherited two hundred thousand pounds of debt from Mary. And she had to have money for unexpected challenges—like the cost of war.

Elizabeth hated spending money. But she needed an extravagant coronation to send a message to those who opposed her. To English Catholics, and many foreigners, Elizabeth was not the true queen. They wanted another Mary—Mary Stuart, Queen of Scots—a Catholic, to rule England. Elizabeth had to spend money to appear queenly. Elizabeth also had to spend money to control rebellions that could destroy her reign.

Stopping rebellions was expensive. Elizabeth, like every other Tudor ruler, did not have a standing army she could call upon whenever she needed it. The only military always on duty were the Yeomen of the Guard, who protected royalty. So if Elizabeth needed soldiers, she hired mercenaries (soldiers who fought for anyone who would pay) or asked her subjects for help.

Elizabeth used soldiers to support Protestants in Scotland, which shares the island of Great Britain with England. Religious and political battles threatened to disrupt Scotland and possibly spill south into England. Scottish Protestants, called Calvinists, were in the majority, but Scottish Catholics had help from France, England's longtime enemy. Mary, Queen of Scots, lived in France, where she was betrothed to the future king. If France succeeded in turning Scotland Catholic, Elizabeth's Protestant realm would be at risk. To pay for an army to fight in Scotland, Elizabeth could ask Parliament to levy a tax. (Parliament is the branch of English government made up of nobles and commoners who represent the people.) But asking Parliament for taxes was unpopular. Members of Parliament—and the English people themselves—seldom wanted taxes.

To raise money to pay soldiers, Elizabeth began reforming England's currency. The economy was in crisis. The new frugal queen set about to straighten it out. Two weeks after her coronation, Elizabeth faced her first Parliament. She wanted to talk about money and rebellion. But Parliament had other ideas.

Elizabeth addresses the House of Lords, one of the houses of Parliament.

Chapter **FOUR**

SHE MUST MARRY!

LESS THAN A MONTH AFTER ELIZABETH'S CORONATION, Parliament met. The new queen wanted to talk business. Parliament wanted to talk marriage. Members of Parliament worried about what would happen to England if Elizabeth died without an heir. Since England depended upon dynasties—rulers who descended from one family—Parliament believed it was crucial for Elizabeth to marry and have children.

The queen refused to be told what to do. When the Parliament petitioned her to marry, Elizabeth responded sharply. She took off her coronation ring and flashed it before them, declaring, "Behold . . . the Pledge of this my Wedlock and Marriage with my Kingdom. Every one of you, and as many as are

English-men, are Children and Kinsmen to me." The queen went on to tell Parliament that she would be satisfied if her gravestone read, "A Queen, having reigned for such a time, lived and died a virgin."

The members of Parliament—all men—looked at each other and smiled. They did not take Elizabeth seriously. They had no doubt she would marry. It was her destiny. King Henry VIII had begun considering whom Elizabeth would marry when she was just sixteen months old. As a young girl, Elizabeth had been paraded at court dressed in rich clothes so foreign ambassadors could view her. At least once her clothes were removed so ambassadors could see the young princess was unblemished.

Elizabeth the princess was good marriage material. Elizabeth the queen was the most promising marriage prospect in Europe. She had money, power, and control of a key country. It's no surprise that princes and kings set out to win her hand. By October 1559, a dozen ambassadors were wooing Elizabeth. Her list of foreign suitors included King Philip II of Spain, King Erik XIV of Sweden, Archduke Charles of Austria, and Henry, duke of Anjou (who would later become King Henry III of France, and whose brother, Francis, duke of Alençon, would also court Elizabeth). As the Spanish ambassador wrote to King Philip II, "Everything depends upon the husband this woman may take. If he be a suitable one, religious matters will go on well and the kingdom will remain friendly to your Majesty, but if not, it will all be spoilt."

Elizabeth understood that carrying on courtships was a way to keep peace in Europe. Some people believe that Elizabeth's unmarried state was her greatest political asset. As long as Catholic rulers like those in France and Spain thought they had a chance to wed Elizabeth, they would not attack England. The young queen needed to encourage several suitors at the same time, while not committing too much to any one. Some observers doubted Elizabeth really ever intended to marry anyone. A year after Elizabeth became queen, the Scottish ambassador, Sir James Melville, told her he knew she'd never marry: "Your Majesty thinks that if you were married you would be but Queen of England, and now you are both King and Queen."

"Sweet Robin"

Englishmen were also vying to become king consort, the title given to men who marry a queen. The earl of Arundel, the earl of Devon, and Sir William Pickering were possible king consorts. But the Englishman Elizabeth favored was tall, dark, handsome Robert Dudley. Elizabeth and Dudley, whom she called Sweet Robin, had known each other since childhood. Dudley said, "I have known her better than any man alive since she was eight years old."

The pair, who were born the same year, had much in common. Each had had a parent beheaded. Dudley's father and grandfather were executed for plotting against the throne. The same Cambridge scholar, Roger Ascham, had tutored them at different times. Elizabeth and Dudley both had been imprisoned in the Tower, although in different parts of the big fortress, so they did not see one another. Both tended to be spirited, with flashes of strong temper.

Robert Dudley was Elizabeth's childhood friend. She named him Master of the Horse, in charge of the royal stables, when she became queen.

THE ROLE OF WOMEN

When Elizabeth became queen, no one expected that she would rule the country for long. Most English people—men and women—did not think women were fit to rule. Elizabeth's sister, Mary, had been queen but had married quickly, as was expected. Royal women were supposed to marry and produce heirs, preferably males. As Mary's widower, Philip II of Spain believed that Elizabeth should marry him "to relieve her of those labors which are only fit for men."

Males were valued far more than females. In Tudor England, it was traditional to send a condolence note to women who gave birth to a girl. Still, women in sixteenth century England had more freedom than did women in other European countries. But freedom depended as much upon money and class as gender. Upper-class girls learned to read and write in English and often in Latin and other Romance languages. Poor or lower-class girls did not learn to read and write. Instead, they likely went to work as servants, doing housework in rich people's homes or inns.

The seemingly endless list of women's work included overseeing apprentices or servants, spinning and weaving wool, making and washing the family clothes, and going to market for food and other items. Women also had responsibility for cooking all meals, cleaning the house, and, of course, taking caring of children.

A woman might have anywhere from eight to fifteen children, about half of whom would likely die young. Many women died giving birth because there was no good medical help or hygiene.

Still, for all their ability to work and run the home, women were considered weak. They were considered less intelligent and more likely to sin than men were. Churches blamed women for the sin that forced Adam and Eve (the Bible's first humans) out of the Garden of Eden.

When Elizabeth became queen, she named Dudley her Master of the Horse. He would be in charge of her safety when she was out of the castle riding. Dudley gave her Irish ponies because they were fast, and Elizabeth relished racing. Elizabeth, who had nicknames for most of the people close to her, called Dudley Eyes, perhaps because his were beautiful and slanted. And also, Dudley was supposed to see all. Another nickname Dudley had was Gypsy, partly because of his dark coloring, but also because many people considered him less than honorable.

By 1559 rumors were swirling around Europe that Elizabeth and Dudley were lovers, though Dudley was married to a woman named Amy Robsart. The couple had married in 1550 when Dudley was almost seventeen, and Elizabeth had been at the wedding. But Dudley was often at court, by Elizabeth's side, while Amy was at home. It was common for most of the one hundred and seventy-five or so courtiers to keep their families at home. There simply wasn't room at court for all of them. Amy Robsart was also sick, with what was probably breast cancer.

By February 1560, Elizabeth had sent a clear message to one suitor that she did not plan to marry. She wrote Swedish king Erik, one of her most persistent suitors, that "we shall never accept or choose any absent husband, how powerful and wealthy a Prince soever... we do not conceive in our heart to take a husband but highly commend this single life...."

While Elizabeth championed the single life, some of her suitors found other brides. When Elizabeth refused to marry Philip II of Spain, he became betrothed to a thirteen-year-old French princess, also named Elizabeth.

During a jousting tournament to celebrate Philip's betrothal, King Henry II of France was wounded and later died. His son Francis II became king of France, and Francis's wife, Mary Stuart, became queen of both France and Scotland. Mary had been living in France for most of her life and was more French than Scottish. Her mother, a Frenchwoman, ruled Scotland for her. Both were Catholic, like most French people, but most Scots were not. In 1560 England and Scotland signed the Treaty of Edinburgh, expelling the French from Scotland. That treaty ensured Scotland would be a Protestant country, which was essential to Elizabeth. At this point, Scotland and England were Protestant, and Elizabeth's strongest Catholic foes— France and Spain—were more closely allied.

Then in September 1560, Amy Robsart, Dudley's wife, was found dead at the bottom of a staircase, her neck broken. Many suspected Dudley had killed his wife so he could marry Elizabeth. The queen immediately ordered Dudley to leave court. To this day, no one knows if Dudley had anything to do with his wife's death. Cancer may have weakened Amy's bones so greatly that she may indeed have broken her neck by falling. An inquest found Dudley not guilty, but his reputation was stained. After the inquest, Elizabeth allowed her favorite Eyes to return to court, and she gave him a room next to hers. Cecil warned Elizabeth that if she married Dudley, her good name would suffer.

Although the laws said people could have their ears or tongues cut off, or be imprisoned or even killed for gossiping, rumors continued about Elizabeth and her Sweet Robin. Still, one time when Dudley tried to order Elizabeth's servants to do something for him, she snapped, "I will have a mistress here and no master."

A few months after Amy died, another death would shake Elizabeth's security. In December 1560, King Francis II of France died suddenly of an ear infection, leaving Mary Stuart a widow. His younger brother was named king, with his mother as regent. Since Mary Stuart's mother, who had been running Scotland for her while she lived in France, had also died, Mary, Queen of Scots, would have to return to Scotland, which she had left when she was just five years old.

By August 1561, Mary was back in Scotland, claiming she was also the rightful queen of England. Some of the same rulers who had courted Elizabeth now turned their attention to the new widow. The king of Sweden, Archduke Charles, and Philip's heir, Don Carlos of Spain, were among Mary's suitors.

Women ruled both England and Scotland, and a third woman, Catherine de Médicis, was the regent guiding France while the young king, Charles IX, grew up. A

This sixteenth century map of Great Britain shows England to the south and Scotland (Scotia) to the north. Ireland is the separate island to the west.

Protestant leader in Scotland, John Knox, lashed out against women in power. He wrote a pamphlet called "First Blast of the Trumpet Against the Monstrous Regiment [government] of Women." Knox called for people to assassinate at least one queen—Mary.

The two cousin queens, Elizabeth and Mary, planned to meet at York. Mary had her eye on Elizabeth's throne. Elizabeth wanted to make sure Mary did not marry a Catholic Spaniard or Frenchman. But Elizabeth had to cancel the planned meeting after Catholics in France massacred some seven thousand Huguenots (French Protestants). Instead of talking with the Catholic Mary, Elizabeth planned to send six thousand troops to help the Huguenots fight the French Catholic government, which was led by Mary's former mother-in-law, Catherine de Médicis.

NEAR DEATH

But in October 1562, before Elizabeth could sign the order to send English soldiers to France, she was struck down with smallpox, an often fatal infectious disease. Elizabeth's temperature rose and she became unconscious. Her council thought she would die. When Elizabeth regained consciousness, her councillors begged her to name a successor. Elizabeth dictated her will, naming Dudley Lord Protector of England. She bequeathed him twenty thousand pounds a year, plus more for his servants. She gave the groomsman who slept in Dudley's room five hundred pounds a year. The generous bequest seemed like a bribe to keep the groom quiet, though Elizabeth swore that although she loved Dudley, they had never been lovers.

Three days later, as she recovered, the queen nullified

her will and named Dudley a privy councillor. He would join Cecil and her other top advisors. Elizabeth stayed in her room for some time, waiting for the rash left by the smallpox to heal. It's likely she was at least somewhat scarred by the pox. Dudley's sister, Lady Mary Sidney, who nursed Elizabeth, became infected and was so badly scarred that she left court and never appeared there in public again. The smallpox also caused the queen's hair to fall out. After that, she began wearing wigs.

The queen's near death terrified her council. They would lose their place at court if Elizabeth died. And without a Protestant successor, the country could fall into civil war. Privately, Elizabeth admitted that Mary, Queen of Scots, was her "next kinswoman." But Elizabeth never publicly named Mary her successor.

Fear of a Catholic queen sparked Parliament once again to talk to Elizabeth about marriage. In January 1563, members of the House of Commons, and then the House of Lords—the two houses of Parliament— petitioned the queen to marry. And once again, Elizabeth was outraged that others were trying to run her life and tell her, a monarch, what to do. The pressure to marry would continue for years—as would Elizabeth's determination to decide her own fate.

The ermine (the animal on Elizabeth's left arm) in this painting represents purity and chastity. The portrait is believed to have been painted in 1585, when Elizabeth was fifty-two years old.

Chapter **FIVE**

STRIFE ABROAD, DANGER AT HOME

ELIZABETH'S MARRIAGE STRUGGLES WERE ONE OF several challenges she faced. Six years after becoming queen, she was confronted with renewed troubles at home—and abroad.

The French religious civil war had proved costly to England. French Catholics defeated the Protestant Huguenots, but the deaths didn't end there. When the English troops returned home, they brought back the bubonic plague, a deadly disease spread by infected fleas on rats. Some rural areas saw twenty thousand deaths. In London alone, approximately three thousand people a week died during the plague outbreak. By the time it ended, the plague had killed about seventeen thousand Londoners.

During the plague in London, a town crier tells the people to bring out the dead.

A TITLE FOR DUDLEY

In 1563, when Parliament again pushed Elizabeth to marry, no one was pushing harder than Robert Dudley. The queen's favorite was shrewd enough to have someone else—Alexander Nowell, the dean of Saint

Paul's Cathedral—make the case for why Elizabeth must marry. It's clear Dudley wanted Elizabeth to marry him. At one point, she promised to make him an earl, a title of the nobility, but then she tore up the orders.

Although she could be persistent and determined, Elizabeth also often could seem indecisive. Changing her mind kept her councillors on edge. When she would say she was going out, then change her mind, it was harder for plotters to know her schedule and habits. But the frequent changes of mind were difficult for those around her.

Dudley was no doubt pained by the queen's indecision about him, but finally, in 1564, Elizabeth made him the earl of Leicester. From that point on, he would be known as Leicester. Some people thought becoming an earl was the first step toward becoming royal consort, the queen's husband. But Elizabeth had other plans.

She was most concerned about finding a suitable groom for her widowed cousin Mary. The Scottish queen, almost a decade younger than Elizabeth, had made it clear she wanted a new husband. If Mary chose a Spaniard or Frenchman, those enemies of England would be a step closer to threatening Elizabeth's throne. Mary and other Catholics believed she was the true queen of England. Elizabeth's Catholic enemies would be happy to help Mary displace her Protestant cousin.

MARY, QUEEN OF SCOTS

The fate of two cousins, both queens, would be intertwined for years, yet their lives were tremendously different. Elizabeth would rule, often wisely, for more than four decades. Her cousin would rule for just six years—a reign and life cut short by reckless choices.

The cousins shared Tudor blood. Elizabeth's father, Henry VIII, was the brother of Mary's grandmother, Margaret Tudor, who married King James IV of Scotland.

Mary's father, James V, died just weeks after her birth in 1542. By the time she was five, Mary was sent to France, already betrothed to the king's son, Francis. For a time, Mary's French Catholic mother, Mary of Guise, ran Scotland until her daughter was old enough to be queen.

Mary stayed in France until her young husband, King Francis, died suddenly. The nineteen-year-old widow had no choice but to return to a country she barely knew. She married Lord Henry Darnley but soon realized the marriage was a mistake; he was jealous of her Italian secretary, David Riccio. One night, while Mary and Riccio were having dinner, Darnley and his men burst in and stabbed Riccio more than sixty times. Mary was six months pregnant when she saw her friend murdered.

After Mary's son, James, was born, she began spending more time with her Lord Admiral, the earl of Bothwell. In 1567 the house Darnley was staying in was blown up. His body was found, two hundred feet from the explosion, but he hadn't died from the blast. Instead, he had been strangled. Many Scots blamed Mary and Bothwell for Darnley's death. Shortly afterward, the queen married Bothwell. Scots were outraged. They thought their young queen had married her husband's killer. Mobs screamed, "Burn the whore!" Two months later, on July 24, 1567,

Scottish rebels forced Mary to abdicate her throne. After being imprisoned for eleven months, the hated former queen escaped.

Never again would she see Bothwell, who fled to Denmark, where he went insane. Never again would she see her son, whom she had last seen a month before his first birthday. Never again would she see Scotland.

Mary, Queen of Scots

Elizabeth wanted a role in deciding whom Mary should marry. Once she had made him an earl, Elizabeth offered Leicester as a husband for the Scottish queen. Elizabeth promised her cousin that if she chose a husband Elizabeth approved of, Mary would be the next queen of England. Neither Mary nor Leicester was interested.

In 1566 Parliament again met to pressure their queen to marry. This time, the House of Commons tried to tie Elizabeth's marriage to how much money they would give her. The ploy failed. The thirty-three-year-old ruler criticized those who dared try to determine her life, comparing England to a body, with herself the head and Parliament the feet. Elizabeth was firm. She, the head, would decide her future and that of the country. "Though I be a woman, I have as good a courage . . . as ever my father had. I am your anointed queen," the angry monarch told Parliament. "I will never be by violence constrained to do anything. I thank God I am endowed with such qualities that if I were turned out of the realm in my petticoat, I were able to live in any place in Christendom."

But the pressure on Elizabeth only grew. On July 29, 1565, Mary married a Scottish Catholic, Henry Stewart, Lord Darnley. He was also her cousin and so had ties to the Tudor throne. Less then a year later, Mary gave birth to a son, James Stuart. Elizabeth was the baby's godmother. Scotland had a coveted male heir. England, under Elizabeth, had none. But Mary's life was far from smooth. Her brief marriage to Darnley ended badly, as did a third, even shorter marriage. By then, Scotland had had enough of Mary Stuart, and she was forced from the throne.

When Mary fled to England, Elizabeth faced a dilemma. If she helped Scottish Protestants and sent Mary back to them, Elizabeth would be undermining a sister queen. If she let Mary stay freely in England, Mary would, without question, plot to take over the throne. Elizabeth opted to keep her cousin under house arrest, but Mary still managed to plot.

Elizabeth had grown thin and careworn, with many worries aside from her ambitious cousin. In December 1568, international troubles flared. After English pirates stole Spanish treasure ships in the Caribbean Sea, Spain seized English ships in the Netherlands, a key market for England's biggest export, wool.

Elizabeth responded by sending seven thousand troops to the Netherlands to help Protestants there rebuff Spanish rule. Spain would continue to control the Netherlands for several more years, but Dutch Protestants began gaining strength. Spain and its Dutch merchants suffered when England began selling wool in Hamburg (Germany) and that only increased tensions between England and Spain.

In early 1569, Elizabeth learned that Mary was secretly planning her fourth marriage, this time to the duke of Norfolk, a Catholic, who was the highest-ranking and richest man in England. Leicester was in on the plans. When he confessed to Elizabeth that Mary's marriage was conditional on her supporting the Protestant church in Scotland, the queen forgave Leicester. Norfolk faced treason charges, yet Elizabeth freed him once he pledged not to have any further contact with Mary.

NORTHERN REBELLION

At midnight on November 9, 1569, Elizabeth faced a more serious threat. A group of earls in northern England, a Catholic stronghold, planned a coup (uprising) to put Mary on the English throne. They led some one thousand horsemen and four thousand foot soldiers.

Elizabeth sent twelve thousand soldiers loyal to her to put down the Northern Rebellion. Most of the earls who led the uprising escaped to Scotland or the Netherlands. But the aftermath was gruesome. Elizabeth's forces, seeking revenge, hanged approximately six hundred people. Her troops destroyed peasants' crops and livestock and tortured villagers.

The following year, 1570, Pope Pius V excommunicated Elizabeth, "the pretended Queen of England and those heretics adhering to her." She was officially no longer a member of the Catholic Church, and Catholics had official permission to rebel against, or even assassinate, the queen. But the pope's harsh stance against Elizabeth strengthened her standing at home. Her Protestant subjects rallied around their

Pope Pius V, leader of the Roman Catholic Church, excommunicated Elizabeth in 1570.

beleaguered ruler. England began celebrating Elizabeth's Accession Day, November 17, the anniversary of when she became queen, as a national holiday, complete with tournaments, banquets, and tolling bells. The holiday would be celebrated for the rest of Elizabeth's reign.

ANOTHER UPRISING
In 1571 an Italian banker named Roberto di Ridolfi, who worked in London, launched another plot to

King Philip II of Spain had been married to Queen Mary I of England. After her death, he schemed all his life to return England to Catholicism.

unseat Elizabeth. Ridolfi wanted to organize a Spanish invasion of England, and he received the pope's promise of support. Ridolfi also enlisted the wealthy duke of Norfolk, who agreed to lead the rebellion in England if Spain sent ten thousand troops.

But Elizabeth's spies uncovered the scheme and evidence that King Philip II was involved. Elizabeth ordered the Spanish ambassador to leave her court in January 1572. Relations between the two European powers were continuing to unravel.

Norfolk was charged with treason on January 16, 1572. The treason trial for England's premier noble would last for hours—far longer than most trials. Despite his popularity, Norfolk was found guilty. Still, Elizabeth was reluctant to kill him. Her councillors and Parliament demanded Norfolk be executed. They viewed the duke's involvement in the Ridolfi plot as a serious threat to Elizabeth's reign and safety. The House of Commons wanted Norfolk's fellow plotter Mary, Queen of Scots, to die as well. As they saw it, she was "the monstrous and huge dragon," while Norfolk was "the roaring lion." Elizabeth refused to kill her cousin but bowed to the pressure and ordered Norfolk's death. After canceling Norfolk's execution three times, Elizabeth finally allowed the popular duke to be beheaded in June 1572. England had lost its only duke, the highest title under royalty. It was the first execution of a noble in Elizabeth's fourteen years as queen.

Elizabeth knights Sir Francis Drake, one of her leading New World adventurers.

Chapter **SIX**

NEW WORLD, OLD PROBLEMS

WHILE THE IMPRISONED MARY STUART CONTINUED to plot, Elizabeth had other worries to face. For much of her reign, Elizabeth was desperate for money. She needed money to pay for various battles, not to mention the cost of maintaining life at court and the dozens of homes she owned.

Elizabeth, and many others, looked west across the Atlantic Ocean to the New World, a source of riches that all of Europe wanted to control. The New World—North and South America—offered treasures such as gold, silver, and jewels. It also had an abundance of items that were then new and exotic in Europe. Europeans coveted New World tobacco, dyes, potatoes, turkey, chocolate, and sugar. All of those goods brought large profits.

Slavery was another way to make money. Elizabeth had already bought shares in John Hawkins's slaving expeditions. In 1562 he sailed to Africa, took three hundred people as slaves, and sold them for great profit in Hispaniola, the island shared by Haiti and the Dominican Republic in modern times. Elizabeth knew about, and benefited from, the early sale of slaves in the New World.

Map of the New World as it was known in the sixteenth century

But even the large profits from slavery couldn't erase the economic pressure at home. In 1572 Parliament passed laws to help support the growing number of poor people. Elizabeth was grateful she could turn to loyal advisors like William Cecil to help her. In 1572 she named him Lord High Treasurer and gave him a title. From then on, he was Lord Burghley.

The next year, Francis Walsingham became principal secretary of state. Walsingham would be Elizabeth's chief spymaster. He had spent years in Europe and had many contacts throughout the continent. Over time, Walsingham placed more than seventy agents and spies around various European courts. Walsingham made sure Elizabeth knew what was happening in other countries, and his spies kept him informed about plots against the queen.

Walsingham's spies updated Elizabeth about the political and religious pressures convulsing Europe. In France religious tension exploded on August 24, 1572, when French Catholics once again launched an assault against Huguenots, the French Protestants. Hundreds were killed in what was known as the St. Bartholomew's Day Massacre. Two years later, in 1574, the French king Charles IX died. Throughout her long rule, Elizabeth was lucky that a number of her enemies died before they could grow stronger. As Walsingham wrote after another Catholic ruler, Don John of Austria, died in 1576, "God dealeth most lovingly with her Majesty, in taking away her enemies."

Elizabeth did not lack for powerful enemies. The pope had already divided the New World between Spain and Portugal, leaving England and France without a claim to America's riches. Still, Elizabeth and her people were determined to reap a share of the treasure. Elizabeth allowed English sailors to attack Spanish ships laden with riches. The English seafarers called themselves privateers. In fact, they were pirates who had the queen's permission to steal. In 1577 Elizabeth gave quiet approval to a young Englishman named Francis Drake, who set out to sail around the world. In 1578 she gave Sir Humphrey Gilbert a patent to settle a colony in the New World.

THE QUEEN AND HER FROG

In 1578, while Drake and Gilbert canvassed the globe, Elizabeth explored the possibility of marriage. The queen was forty-five years old. If she was to give birth to an heir, she had to marry quickly. She renewed a courtship with a Frenchman, Francis, duke of Alençon. She called him the Frog. He was the younger brother of the new French king, Henry III. Alençon was twenty-one years younger than Elizabeth. He was short, with a big nose and a face scarred by smallpox. Elizabeth found him charming.

While the queen and her Frog were courting, the queen's former suitor, Leicester, secretly married. Elizabeth and Leicester's love had settled into friend-

Elizabeth considered marriage to Francis, duke of Alençon, but her subjects were opposed to the idea.

ship years ago. Still, the queen was livid about Leicester's marriage to Lettice Knollys. She had given him many titles and honors, and the two had maintained their friendship for decades. It seems clear that Elizabeth loved Leicester far more than most English people did. An anonymous book, called *Leycester's Commonwealth,* published in 1584, called him "the most hated man in England." The book accused Leicester of seducing many women and killing rivals.

If many of the English were convinced that Leicester was not good enough for their Virgin Queen, many more feared their pure Elizabeth would marry a foreigner. The queen's serious marriage talks with the Frog sparked great concern among her advisors and subjects. She turned to her Privy Council for advice. Seven councillors—including Leicester and Walsingham—opposed the marriage, while Burghley and four others supported the Frenchman. When her advisors asked Elizabeth what she wanted, she broke down crying. The queen had wanted a clear signal that she could marry her Frog.

In 1579 a lawyer and landowner named John Stubbes published a pamphlet denouncing Elizabeth's French duke. Stubbes was a Puritan, a Protestant who opposed all things Catholic. Stubbes did not want his queen to marry a Catholic, even though the Frog was sympathetic toward Protestants. Stubbes wrote that Elizabeth was like "a lamb to the slaughter"—the slaughter being marriage to the French duke. The pamphlet said Alençon had sinister motives for marrying a woman decades older, and that Elizabeth was too old to be able to give birth to a child safely. Elizabeth was enraged. She hated attacks on her right to rule and to rule her own life. She sent the Puritan, his printer, and his publisher to the Tower to be hanged. Legally, though, Elizabeth did not have the right to execute them. So, after pardoning the printer, she ordered that Stubbes and his publisher have their right hands chopped off. When Stubbes lost his hand, he used his left hand to doff his hat, saying "God save the Queen!" before he passed out.

THE SEA DOG TRIUMPHS

In 1580, three years after he set sail, Francis Drake returned from his voyage around the world. He'd lost four of his five ships, and most of his surviving

Sir Francis Drake's fleet attacking a Spanish treasure ship

sailors were sick, but Drake brought back immense riches and maps detailing Spain's treasure routes. The man Elizabeth called her Sea Dog had fetched one hundred tons of silver and one hundred pounds by weight of gold. All told, Drake plundered treasures worth four hundred thousand British pounds from Spanish ships.

Elizabeth was delighted to have the much needed wealth, and in April 1581 she knighted Drake. Sir Francis Drake boasted, "No one in the world understood better the art of sailing." The Spanish ambassador called Drake "the master thief of the unknown world." Spain was incensed that Elizabeth had rewarded a pirate. Tensions continued to rise between the two countries.

Good-bye to the Frog

Within England, opposition grew to Elizabeth's plans to marry Alençon. The queen was torn. One day in September 1581, in front of a crowded gallery at court, Elizabeth kissed her Frog, said she would marry him, and gave him a ring from her finger. The next day, she announced she had changed her mind. It seems Elizabeth cared too much for her people's goodwill to anger them. In February 1582, the Frenchman left England, sailing home a richer man with Elizabeth's parting gift of ten thousand pounds. After her Frog left, Elizabeth wrote this poem:

I grieve and dare not show my discontent.
I love and yet am forced to seem to hate.
I do, yet dare not say I ever meant.
I seem stark mute yet inwardly do prate [talk].
I am and not, I freeze and yet am burned
Since from myself another self I turned.

At age forty-eight, Elizabeth said good-bye to the one man she may have intended to marry. Younger men would continue to flirt with the powerful queen. They wanted her favors—power, titles, and rights to tax goods like wine and wool for profit—but not her love.

POLITICAL PROBLEMS

The duke of Alençon used Elizabeth's love money to fight the Spanish troops occupying the Netherlands. Elizabeth and other Protestants continued to back Dutch Protestants who struggled to free themselves of Spain's Catholic rule.

On June 10, 1584, Alençon died in the Netherlands. For three weeks, Elizabeth cried every day. The affair between the queen and her Frog had ended two years before, but she was saddened by his death, and the strife in the Low Countries dragged on.

Life in England was not easy either. In 1584 Dr. William Parry, one of Walsingham's former spies and a member of the House of Commons, was arrested for plotting to kill the queen. That year Parliament passed a law called the Act of Association, which punished anyone who plotted to dethrone Elizabeth. The law was intended to thwart Mary, Queen of Scots, still conspiring against her cousin. Mary's son, James, who had been raised by his Protestant uncle, had succeeded to Scotland's throne in 1578, when he was twelve. Mary's only chance to rule was as queen of England.

A NEW WORLD SETTLEMENT

In 1584 Sir Humphrey Gilbert disappeared at sea during an attempt to settle a New World colony. Elizabeth decided to give Gilbert's half brother permission to try. The half brother was Walter Ralegh. He was tall and handsome and knew how to charm the queen. Elizabeth did not want Ralegh, who had become her favorite courtier, to sail halfway across the world. So although he had the royal patent for a colony, Ralegh was ordered to stay at court while his men set sail for the New World. Their voyage began on April 27, 1584. On July 13, Ralegh's captains had landed in what is now known as North Carolina's Outer Banks. They claimed that land for Elizabeth and for England. When the ships returned, Ralegh was delighted to hear the captains' tales of this new land. To honor Elizabeth, the Virgin Queen, Ralegh named the land Virginia, though it was already called Ossomocomuck by the Algonquin Indians who lived there.

It's likely that lands other than Virginia were on the queen's mind. In 1585 Spain had sent its best army to the Netherlands. Elizabeth responded by sending Leicester there to lead English troops against Spain. Two of Europe's most powerful countries—England and Spain—were then at war in a third country. Elizabeth abhorred war. She hated soldiers' loss of life; she hated her loss of control when she had to hand power over to men to run the military; and she hated the cost of war, which inevitably drained the English treasury. Still, the queen knew at times war was necessary. England would be in danger if Spain continued to grow stronger.

While soldiers battled in the Netherlands, seven English ships, carrying somewhere between five hundred and one thousand men, set sail on April 9, 1585, for Ralegh's Virginia. Most were going for the adventure and the chance to capture Spanish treasure and quickly return to England. Only one hundred and nine men would stay on Roanoke Island through the winter. They were not truly prepared to settle a colony. Instead, they mapped and explored, took notes, and ended up mistreating and alienating the Indians who had befriended them. On June 18, 1586, Sir Francis Drake arrived to find the Roanoke colony failing. When storms hit, Drake quickly departed, taking Ralegh's would-be settlers with him. Three settlers who were away from the ship were left behind in the rush to beat the storm. England's first colony had

Roanoke Island, site of the first Virginia colony

been less than promising. But Ralegh and others would try again.

MARY'S LAST PLOT

By 1586 Mary Stuart had been a prisoner in England for eighteen years. During that time, she'd smuggled countless letters to supporters throughout Europe, describing plans to take Elizabeth's place. Walsingham, Elizabeth's spymaster, laid a trap to catch Mary scheming. She had found a brewer who had agreed to smuggle a series of letters in a beer keg. Walsingham intercepted Mary's letters, which revealed a new plot with an Englishman named Anthony Babington to kill

Elizabeth and seize the throne. In September Babington and six other conspirators were executed. Traitors suffered a horrible death. They were drawn, hanged, and quartered. That means their kidneys and intestines were cut out while they were still alive, then after being hanged to death, their bodies were cut into pieces.

On October 11, 1586, a commission of peers and privy councillors met at Fotheringay Castle, where Mary was being held, to decide the Scotswoman's fate. The evidence showed Mary's guilt, in her own handwriting, calling for Elizabeth's death. On October 29, Parliament demanded Mary's head. Elizabeth still did not want to kill her cousin. She asked Parliament for a lesser punishment for Mary. It was refused. Elizabeth asked what her enemies would think "when it shall be spread, that for the safety of herself a maiden Queen could be content to spill the blood, even of her own kinswoman?" Despite Elizabeth's hesitations, Parliament was adamant. Mary must die.

On February 1, 1587, Elizabeth signed her cousin's death warrant. One week later, on February 8, Mary was beheaded. Back in London, Elizabeth was grief-stricken. She could not eat or sleep. The queen of England had killed another queen, her own cousin.

The English fleet battles the Spanish Armada.

Chapter **SEVEN**

WAR

MARY'S EXECUTION ENRAGED CATHOLICS, BUT before she died, Mary passed her claim to England's throne to another Catholic ruler, King Philip of Spain. Spain began preparations to go to war against England and seize power from Elizabeth, the heretic queen.

Then, two months after Mary's death, on April 19, 1587, Sir Francis Drake sailed into Cádiz harbor in Spain, surprising the Spanish navy. Twenty-four English ships demolished more than that number of Spanish vessels, along with Spain's supply of barrel staves. The staves were essential items for making the casks that stored food and water onboard ships. After burning the port, Drake captured one hundred thousand pounds' worth of Spanish treasure. The brash Englishman boasted that all he did was "singe the King of Spain's beard," but Drake's stealth attack delayed Philip's military plans by more than a year. That gave England crucial time to bolster its tiny fleet.

Elizabeth was so delighted with Drake's daring that

Sir Francis Drake, above, attacked Cádiz, Spain, which delayed Philip II's plans to send his Armada to England.

she rode her horse up stairs in a fit of joy. England at that time had nowhere near the military strength of Spain. By the 1580s, Philip controlled 20 percent of western Europe and 25 percent of its people. Beyond that were the Spanish conquests in Mexico, Peru, the Philippines, and parts of Africa and Asia. Spain's Armada, its vast fleet of ships, was considered invincible—unbeatable. Philip could count on the New World's riches to pay for war. He also had the backing of the pope, who pledged money to Spain as soon as that Catholic country invaded England.

Elizabeth did not have anyone as powerful as the pope behind her. She depended upon privateers—her official pirates—to raid Spanish treasure ships. England had more gunpowder than Spain, but its greatest resource was its daring seamen. Spaniards were terrified of Sir Francis Drake, whom they called El Draque—the Dragon. Elizabeth named Drake, Sir Walter Ralegh, and Sir Martin Frobisher to lead the Royal Commission to prepare England's navy for war. The Royal Navy had just thirty-four fighting ships, but that number quickly grew to two hundred as the country enlisted private ships for everything from scouting to carrying supplies. England was ready for war.

BATTLING THE ARMADA
On July 19, 1588, 130 Spanish ships commanded by the duke of Medina-Sidonia were sighted off the English coast at Cornwall. Legend has it that Sir Francis

Drake and the navy's Lord Admiral, Charles Howard, were playing a game of lawn bowling near the port of Plymouth when they learned that the Armada had been sighted. Drake, ever the confident Sea Dog, supposedly said, "We have time enough to finish the game and beat the Spaniards, too."

By July 21, just over one hundred English ships were positioned for battle. Spain had about 125 warships "with lofty turrets like castles" lined up in an imposing crescent formation. Philip's massive ships were weighted down with horses and some seventeen thousand troops. Spain planned to march into England and take control after defeating the English navy. The English ships, smaller and faster than those of the invincible Armada, held just fifteen hundred troops, with more English on shore to defend there if necessary.

The naval skirmishes continued until July 27, when the Armada reached the neutral French port of Calais. There the Spanish navy planned to link up with its army, led by the duke of Parma. But Parma's soldiers were delayed, and the next day England went on the offensive. Eight small English ships filled with wood and gunpowder headed toward the Armada. As they neared the Spanish fleet, the English crew set their ships afire, jumped overboard, and swam away. Then the burning English ships sailed, unmanned, into Spain's fleet. When the Spanish ships rushed to escape England's "hellburners," Spain's invincible crescent formation was broken.

Ark Royal, *the English flagship in the sea battle against the Spanish Armada*

The next morning, July 28, a fiery sea battle raged for nine hours, during which approximately one thousand Spaniards died. Finally, the English ran out of ammunition and retreated. England had not lost a single ship. What was left of the tattered Armada straggled away into the wind-whipped North Sea.

ELIZABETH'S COURAGE

Elizabeth and all of England feared Spain would also attempt a land attack. The queen had declared she would lead her army herself. Her Privy Council refused to allow that. Leicester explained, "Your person being the most dainty and sacred thing we have in this world to care for, a man must trouble when he thinks of it . . . I cannot, most dear Queen, consent to that, for upon your well-being consists all the safety of your whole kingdom and therefore preserve that all above."

Elizabeth stayed in London during the battle. Still, ten days later, with England still tensed for a possible Spanish attack, the queen went to speak to her soldiers at Tilbury, near London. Riding a white horse, dressed in white velvet adorned with silver armor, Elizabeth rallied her troops with one of her most famous speeches. "I know I have the body of a weak and feeble woman, but I have the heart and stomach of a king, and of a king of England, too, and think foul scorn that Parma or Spain, or any prince of Europe should dare to invade the borders of my realm."

The feared attack by the duke of Parma, or any Spaniard, never happened. Instead, storms off the coast of Scotland and Ireland destroyed dozens more Spanish ships. By the time the Armada returned to Spain, it had lost nearly half its fleet. England's Royal Navy had defeated the invincible Spanish Armada.

To Spain, the Armada's loss was merely a setback. Philip would build new ships and continue to harass England. But to Elizabeth and her countrymen, defeating the Armada was an immense victory. Spain's grip on Europe began to loosen. The Low Countries, chafing under Spanish rule, mocked the invincible Armada. In the long run, England would gain control of the seas, remaining the dominant navy for three centuries. But the immediate result of England's proud victory was that England would remain free of a Catholic ruler. Elizabeth would live to rule for years to come.

In this painting, known as the Rainbow Portrait, Elizabeth holds a rainbow, which symbolizes the brightness of her enlightened reign.

Chapter **EIGHT**

GRIEF AT HOME AND BEYOND

ELIZABETH HAD SCANT TIME TO SAVOR HER ARMADA victory. In September 1588, just months after the battle, her longtime friend Leicester became ill with stomach pain, exhaustion, and fever. He left court to go home to Kenilworth. On the way, he died. When she heard, Elizabeth shut herself in her room and stayed there until William Cecil, Lord Burghley, ordered the door broken down.

Elizabeth treasured Leicester's final letter to her, written shortly before his death. When she died years later, it was found with her most precious things in a pearl-encrusted box by her bed. She had written "His last letter" on the note.

The queen had already named Leicester's stepson,

the earl of Essex, as her Master of the Horse. Essex, whom the queen nicknamed Wild Horse, was one of the new generation of young nobles who would vie for the monarch's attention and gifts. The young bloods began replacing Elizabeth's loyal but aging advisors. Elizabeth remained strong and relatively healthy but plagued by money problems and international strife.

MORE MONEY PROBLEMS

In February 1589, Parliament reluctantly agreed to a stunning double tax that barely covered the cost of the Armada war. Later that year, when King Henry III of France, a Catholic, was assassinated, Elizabeth rushed troops to support the new Protestant king there. To pay for soldiers, Elizabeth once again looked to her seaworthy pirates. Sir Francis Drake led an expedition to crush the last of Spain's Armada. The queen contributed money and ships, hoping for another gargantuan profit. Instead, the Sea Dog's voyage foundered, capturing just one Spanish ship. At least eight thousand members of Drake's fleet died, mostly of disease. After the debacle, Drake retired.

In 1590 Elizabeth lost two trusted members of her Privy Council—Lord Chancellor Sir Christopher Hatton and Secretary of State Sir Francis Walsingham, her spymaster. By the 1590s, Burghley was the only original member of Elizabeth's Privy Council. Elizabeth's longest serving advisor, Sir Spirit, suffered from gout but had trained his son, Robert Cecil, to take his place at court. In 1590 Robert Cecil had begun acting as secretary of state. The younger Cecil was savvy, short, and somewhat hunchbacked. Elizabeth nicknamed him

Robert Cecil trained under his father to become Elizabeth's secretary of state.

Pigmy. Robert Cecil competed with the earl of Essex for power at court. Essex, especially, was jealous and resentful of anyone who had the queen's ear.

Elizabeth sorely needed the guidance of Burghley, his son, and her other councillors. By the mid-1590s, England was suffering severe food shortages, caused by several years of heavy rains that ruined farmers' crops. Many peasants had been forced off their small farm plots, which were converted to sheep pastures when landlords realized they could profit more from wool. Many of those displaced peasants ended up in London, which made the city even more crowded and filthy. People were beginning to starve.

The troubles overseas also continued to worsen. Elizabeth spent three hundred thousand pounds over four years to shore up the new Protestant government in France. She spent another fifty thousand pounds in the Netherlands. But her biggest international problem lay just across the Irish Sea.

Ireland was rising against English rule. In 1595 the Irish earl of Tyrone, Hugh O'Neill, led a rebellion against the English controlling his country. Philip of Spain, still smarting over the Armada defeat, financed the Irish rebellion.

English privateers continued to strike Spanish ships—taking ninety-one Spanish treasure ships in one year alone. Philip was convinced England needed to be defeated. In 1590 Philip had forbidden Spanish ships from sailing the West

Indies trade routes because he did not want to make them easy prey for English ships. The following year, Philip sent more aggressive convoys of ships to protect the Spanish trade routes. But England once again managed to confound the Spaniards by seizing another rich merchant ship. Elizabeth received 141,000 pounds as the crown's share of the plunder. Still the queen needed even more money to pay for her many military interventions. She was forced to sell some of her father's heirlooms, like his gold seal and chains, along with nearly one-fourth of her royal lands for eighty thousand pounds.

During this period, Burghley, Elizabeth's most trusted council member, grew still frailer. He had been unable to walk for some time and needed to be carried about in a chair but had still come to court to aid his queen. Elizabeth's Sir Spirit had served her for four decades. Burghley called her "the wisest woman that ever was, for she understood the interests and dispositions of all the princes in her time, and was so perfect in her knowledge of her own realm, that no councillor she had could tell her anything she did not know before." Their respect was mutual. Elizabeth had written Burghley that "he was to her in all things, and would be, Alpha and Omega"—the beginning and the end. When Burghley lay dying, the queen went to him and fed him soup herself. By year's end, Elizabeth had lost her first and most loyal advisor.

The queen's newer, younger councillors viewed her as old and pitiful and something of a joke. They didn't respect their aging ruler, as had the councillors who had served her earlier. Robert Cecil would say Elizabeth "was more than a man, and in troth [truth], sometimes less than a woman." The sixty-five-year-old monarch still had a sharp mind, but she was aging physically. Her handwriting grew shaky. She stopped writing poetry. Some of her final Latin translations dwell on old age and the fakeness of flatterers. Power struggles began to wrack the court, as advisors squabbled for control. Elizabeth had to intervene to prevent a dual between Essex and Ralegh. Still, Elizabeth found strength to rule.

ESSEX FAILS

In 1599 Elizabeth sent twenty-nine thousand troops to Ireland, under Essex's leadership, to put down the determined Irish. It was the largest army to leave England during all of Elizabeth's reign. But instead of following her orders, Essex signed a temporary truce with rebel leader Hugh O'Neill and returned to London. There he surprised the queen in her chamber, before her makeup and wig were on. Elizabeth listened to Essex's explanations but was not appeased. When the queen refused to renew Essex's lease entitling him to the taxes on sweet imported wines, the thirty-four-year-old nobleman turned sullen. In his last existing letter to the queen, dated

The earl of Essex was one of Elizabeth's young courtiers. He was later executed for treason.

November 17, 1600, he wrote "that being now an old woman," Elizabeth "was no less crooked and distorted in mind than she was in body." In February 1601, Essex led an ill-fated rebellion to seize control of the court and install his friends as advisors to the throne. He was quickly arrested, found guilty of

ELIZABETH THE IMAGE-MAKER

The queen was fifty-five years old when England defeated the Armada, but her age was a forbidden topic. She still saw herself as a young, vigorous queen and expected others to do the same. No image of Elizabeth could be printed without a license. She controlled how she was depicted. She used her idealized image to encourage loyalty. English people wore cameos and medallions engraved with her image, and many homes had at least one likeness of the queen.

Elizabeth's jewels and exaggerated costumes were a form of propaganda to create the queenly image she wanted. In the famous Armada Portrait (see cover), she sits before battle scenes with pearls (symbolizing virginity) dripping from her hair, hanging from her neck, and sewn by the hundreds to her puffy gown. Her face is unlined, unscarred. A more realistic image from that same time can be found on the Armada Jewel, a rare stone brooch that shows an older Elizabeth, with a sharp nose and piercing eyes.

The famous Rainbow Portrait (see page 90) shows a young woman with bright, flowing hair. Yet Elizabeth was nearly sixty when this picture was painted. It shows the monarch as all-seeing,

treason, and executed. Elizabeth began to sink into melancholy.

That same year, Parliament passed the Poor Laws to crack down on rising numbers of vagrants, desperate for food. To help ease the food shortages, the people demanded an end to the system that let all-knowing. The pattern of eyes and ears adorning her orange cloak represents fame and knowledge. The serpent of pearls and rubies embroidered on her sleeve symbolizes wisdom. The rainbow she holds reads, *"Non sine sole iris"* ("No rainbow without the sun"). It is clear that Elizabeth is the sun.

As she aged, Elizabeth continued to try to use her youthful beauty as a symbol of her queenliness. She wore heavy white makeup to hide her smallpox scars and wrinkles. She wore red wigs to cover her gray hair. She donned ornate clothing to distract others from her aging face. As she grew older, she lost many teeth to frequent toothaches and abscesses, and one side of her face became sunken because of it. The queen's remaining teeth were black or decayed. Pictures show her with her mouth closed. People who saw the queen in person knew she was not the youthful beauty her portraits presented. Sir Francis Bacon wrote, "She imagined that the people, who are much influenced by externals, would be diverted by the glitter of her jewels from noticing the decay of her personal attractions." She ordered other women at court to dress plainly so they wouldn't compete with her splendor.

In the end, fancy clothes, elaborate jewels, and glossy wigs couldn't hide the queen's age. But for much of her reign, Elizabeth spent thousands of pounds each year on endless layers of clothes and jewels to create an image of an elegant, powerful queen. And that image remains, long after Elizabeth herself.

nobles control taxes on all kinds of products—from sweet wines to salt and coal. Under pressure, Elizabeth abolished the system, which monarchs had long used to reward courtiers.

Speaking to Parliament, the sixty-eight-year-old ruler gave what may have been the greatest speech of her life. Elizabeth said, "Though God hath raised me high, yet this I account the glory of my crown, that I have reigned with your loves. . . . It is not my desire to live or reign longer than my life and reign shall be for your good. And though you have had, and may have, many mightier and wiser princes sitting in this seat, yet you never had, nor shall have any that will love you better."

A member of Parliament said her speech was worthy to be written in gold. For generations to come, English people would know Elizabeth's Golden Speech. Under Elizabeth, England had grown powerful, had defeated Spain, had saved Scotland for Protestants, and would shortly put down the Irish uprising. Even enemies like Pope Sixtus V admired her, saying, "She is certainly a great Queen and were she only a Catholic she would be our dearly beloved. Just look at how well she governs! She is only a woman, only mistress of half an island, and yet she makes herself feared by Spain, by France, by the Empire, by all."

Yet even strong queens grow weak. By January 1603, the sixty-nine-year-old monarch was failing. She stayed at Richmond, a favorite palace she called her warm nest. There, in her warm nest, Elizabeth rested on cushions on the floor. She refused food or medicine for days. Finally, she was persuaded to go to bed. Early in the morning of March 24, 1603, Queen Elizabeth I died.

Some say that before Elizabeth died, she murmured

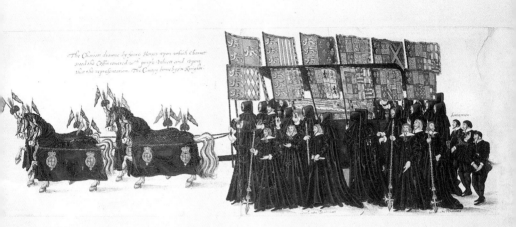

Elizabeth's death was the end of the Tudor dynasty. Her people mourned the passing of an age, as shown in this painting of her funeral procession.

the name of her godson and successor, James VI of Scotland, Mary Stuart's son. When James became king of England, he commanded monuments be built for his mother and for Elizabeth. Elizabeth's effigy is still on display at Westminster Abbey. Like the queen herself, it is imposing, regal, and impossible to take in wholly from one angle. The Virgin Queen, who had been compared to Diana, the Huntress and to Cynthia, the Goddess of the Moon, was dead.

Her glory lives on, in the plays, books, and stories she inspired. And her memory remains, as true as one of the many effigies English villages made in

The effigy of Elizabeth I in Westminster Abbey shows a woman imposing, regal, and complex, even in death.

her honor: "This was she that in despight of death/Lives still ador'd."

ELIZABETH'S LEGACY

The forty-plus years of Elizabeth's reign became known as the Elizabethan Age. Her ability to keep England Protestant, without the kinds of bloody persecutions practiced by her sister Mary in the name of Catholocism, gave England years of stability that allowed the nation to grow and prosper. It was a time of high art—music, theater, and literature flourished under her reign. Glorious mansions were built in her honor. But it was also a time of great cruelty and vulgarity. England profited from slavery. Growing numbers of people, forced off their rural lands, starved and were punished simply because they were poor.

The queen's personal tastes shaped her country's culture. Unlike her predecessors, Elizabeth preferred music and plays to magicians, jugglers, and dancing girls. So troupes of musicians and actors gained a foothold at court. The queen had a choir of fifty singers and forty musicians and her own theater group, The Queen's Company, made up of a dozen actors. Leicester and other nobles also sponsored their own acting troupes. By the end of the sixteenth century, actors were performing in theaters, rather than in the street or in inn yards. Playwrights such as William Shakespeare and Ben Jonson grew prominent. Other writers, including John Donne, Christopher Marlowe, Francis Bacon, and Edmund Spenser flourished during Elizabeth's years.

The Elizabethan Age was a time of great contrasts—a time of intense religious debates and growing profits from slavery; a time of architectural marvels and increasing hunger and poverty; a time of fine art and wretched cruelty. It was an era defined by international victories, led by a woman who never fought or traveled outside her country. The defeat of the Spanish Armada was perhaps Elizabeth's greatest triumph—and yet this queen hated war. In an age of lavish architecture, the queen herself never built any new palaces. It was an opulent time, but Elizabeth was frugal and often desperate for money. It was a time as intense and complicated as the queen whose name it bears.

SOURCES

8   G. B. Harrison, ed., *The Letters of Queen Elizabeth* (London: Cassell and Company Ltd., 1935), 20.

8   Susan Watkins, *In Public and in Private: Elizabeth I and Her World* (London: Thames and Hudson, 1998), 35.

9   Susan Bassnett, *Elizabeth I: A Feminist Perspective* (New York: St. Martin's Press, 1998), 33.

10 Watkins, 48.

13 Denise Dersin, ed., *What Life Was Like in the Realm of Elizabeth: England A.D. 1533–1603* (Alexandria, Virginia: Time-Life Books, 1998), 17.

13 Carolly Erickson, *The First Elizabeth* (New York: St. Martin's Press, 1997), 31.

15 Ibid., 41.

16 Ibid., 47; Ibid., 50.

20 David Starkey, *Elizabeth: The Struggle for the Throne* (New York: HarperCollins, 2001), 85.

21 Watkins, 22.

23 J. E. Neale, *Queen Elizabeth I* (Chicago: Academy of Chicago Publishers, 1999), 19.

24 Erickson, 69.

24 Bassnett, 24.

33 Starkey, 148; Ibid., 150.

34 Jane Resh Thomas, *Behind the Mask: The Life of Queen Elizabeth I* (New York: Clarion Books, 1998), 73.

34 Bassnett, 56.

34 Dersin, 21.

35 Thomas, 69.

35 Bassnett, 35.

35 Thomas, 73.

37–38 Neale, 55.

42 Bassnett, 37.

45–46 Thomas, 95.

46 Karen Lindsey, *Divorced, Beheaded, Survived: A Feminist Reinterpretation of the Wives of Henry VIII* (Reading, MA: Addison-Wesley Publishing Company, 1995), 214.

46–47 Marc Aronson, *Sir Walter Ralegh and the Quest for El Dorado* (New York: Clarion Books, 2000), 27.
47 Lindsey, 215.
47 Watkins, 161.
49 Kenneth O. Morgan, ed., *The Young Oxford History of Britain and Ireland* (Oxford, England: Oxford University Press, 1996), 196.
49 Lindsey, 61.
50 Watkins., 99.
50 Harrison, 32.
52 Morgan, 197.
53 Thomas, 98.
55 Alison Plowden, *The Tudor Women: Queens and Commoners* (New York: Atheneum, 1979), 159.
62 Dersin, 26.
64 Robert Green, *Queen Elizabeth I: A First Book* (Danbury, CT: Franklin Watts, 1997), 223.
67 Neale, 119.
71 Ibid., 242.
74 Bassnett, 43; Dersin, 58.
76 Ibid., 121.
77 Bassnett, 50.
81 Neale, 286.
84 Dersin, 136.
85 Neale, 304.
86 Green, 41.
86 Dersin, 136.
86–87 Morgan, 202.
87–88 Watkins, 177.
88 Morgan, 202.
92 Thomas, 170.
95 Watkins, 190.
95 Neale, 363.
96 Watkins, 190.
96 Neale, 385.
99 Watkins, 78.
99–100 Neale, 400–401.
100 Watkins, 197.
101 Ibid., 194.

BIBLIOGRAPHY

Ashelford, Jane. *The Art of Dress: Clothes and Society, 1500–1914.* New York: Harry N. Abrams, Inc., 1996.

Bassnett, Susan. *Elizabeth I: A Feminist Perspective.* New York: St. Martin's Press, 1998.

Crookston, Peter, ed. *The Ages of Britain.* New York: St. Martin's Press, 1983.

Delderfield, Eric R., ed. *Kings and Queens of England.* New York: Weathervane, 1978.

Erickson, Carolly. *The First Elizabeth.* New York: St. Martin's Press, 1997.

Harrison, G. B., ed. *The Letters of Queen Elizabeth.* London: Cassell and Company Ltd., 1935.

Lace, William W. *Defeat of the Spanish Armada: Battles of the Middle Ages.* San Diego, CA: Lucent Books, 1997.

Lindsey, Karen. *Divorced, Beheaded, Survived: A Feminist Reinterpretation of the Wives of Henry VIII.* Reading, MA: Addison-Wesley Publishing Company, 1995.

Loades, David. *The Tudor Court.* Totowa, NJ: Barnes and Noble Books, 1987.

Meltzer, Milton. *Ten Queens: Portraits of Women of Power.* New York: Dutton Children's Books, 1998.

Morgan, Kenneth O., ed. *The Young Oxford History of Britain and Ireland.* Oxford: Oxford University Press, 1996.

Neale, J. E. *Queen Elizabeth I.* Chicago: Academy of Chicago Publishers, 1999.

Opfell, Olga S. *Queens, Empresses, Grand Duchesses and Regents: Women Rulers of Europe, A.D. 1328–1989.* Jefferson, North Carolina: McFarland & Company, Inc., 1989.

Plowden, Alison. *The Tudor Women: Queens and Commoners.* New York: Atheneum, 1979.

———. *The Young Elizabeth.* New York: Stein and Day, 1971.

Ross, Josephine. *The Tudors: England's Golden Age.* New York: G. P. Putnam's Sons, 1979.

Ross, Stewart. *How It Was: Elizabethan Life.* London: B. T. Batsford Ltd., 1991.

Starkey, David. *Elizabeth: The Struggle for the Throne.* New York: HarperCollins, 2001.
Stepanek, Sally. *Mary, Queen of Scots.* New York: Chelsea House Publishers, 1987.
Watkins, Susan. *In Public and in Private: Elizabeth I and Her World.* London: Thames and Hudson, 1998.
Weir, Alison. *The Life of Elizabeth I.* New York: Ballantine Publishing Group, 1998.
Williamson, David. *Debrett's Kings and Queens of Britain.* Devon, Great Britain: Webb & Bower, 1986.
Woodward, G. W. O. *Queen Elizabeth I: An Illustrated Biography.* London: Pitkin Pictorials Ltd., 1972.

FOR FURTHER READING

Aronson, Marc. *Sir Walter Ralegh and the Quest for El Dorado.* New York: Clarion Books, 2000.

Dersin, Denise, ed. *What Life Was Like in the Realm of Elizabeth: England A.D. 1533–1603.* Alexandria, Virginia: Time-Life Books, 1998.

Green, Robert. *Queen Elizabeth I: A First Book.* Danbury, CT: Franklin Watts, 1997.

Jenkins, Elizabeth. *Elizabeth the Great.* New York: Putnam, 1959.

Thomas, Jane Resh. *Behind the Mask: The Life of Queen Elizabeth I.* New York: Clarion Books, 1998.

WEBSITES

These two websites provide biographies of Queen Elizabeth I, selections from her writings, and portrait galleries.

<http://www.luminarium.org/renfit/eliza.htm>

<http://www.tudorhistory.org/elizabeth/>

INDEX

OTHER TITLES FROM LERNER AND A&E®

Arthur Ashe	Legends of Dracula
The Beatles	Legends of Santa Claus
Benjamin Franklin	Louisa May Alcott
Bill Gates	Madeleine Albright
Bruce Lee	Malcolm X
Carl Sagan	Mark Twain
Chief Crazy Horse	Maya Angelou
Christopher Reeve	Mohandas Gandhi
Daring Pirate Women	Mother Teresa
Edgar Allan Poe	Nelson Mandela
Eleanor Roosevelt	Oprah Winfrey
George W. Bush	Princess Diana
George Lucas	Queen Cleopatra
Gloria Estefan	Queen Latifah
Jack London	Rosie O'Donnell
Jacques Cousteau	Saint Joan of Arc
Jane Austen	Thurgood Marshall
Jesse Owens	Tiger Woods
Jesse Ventura	William Shakespeare
Jimi Hendrix	Wilma Rudolph
John Glenn	Women in Space
Latin Sensations	Women of the Wild West

ABOUT THE AUTHOR

Kate Havelin was in junior high when she decided to be a writer. She edited her high school and college newspapers and studied journalism. After graduating, she worked as a television producer for more than a decade. This is Havelin's ninth book for young readers. She lives with her husband and two sons in St. Paul, Minnesota.

PHOTO ACKNOWLEDGMENTS

The images in this book are used with the permission of: © North Wind Pictures, pp. 2, 41, 80, 82, 84, 87; The Royal Collection © 2001, Her Majesty Queen Elizabeth II, p. 6; Independent Picture Service, p. 9; © Gianni Dagli Orti/CORBIS, p. 11; © National Portrait Gallery, London, pp. 12, 16, 18, 27, 36, 38; © Hulton/Archive, pp. 23, 29, 73, 93; © The Art Archive/Palazzo Farnese Caparola/Dagli Orti, p. 31; © Jonathan Blair/CORBIS, p. 33; © Bettmann/CORBIS, pp. 40, 56, 58, 66, 70, 75; © Hulton-Deutsch Collection/CORBIS, p. 44; © Wallace Collection, London, UK/Bridgeman Art Library, p. 48; © Giraudon/Art Resource, NY, pp. 53, 65; © Archivo Iconografico, S.A./CORBIS, pp. 61, 90; © Baldwin H. Ward & Kathryn C. Ward/CORBIS, p. 68; © National Trust/Art Resource, NY, p. 97; © Art Resource, NY, p. 101; © Angelo Hornak/CORBIS, p. 102.

Front cover, © National Portrait Gallery, London/Superstock
Back cover, © National Portrait Gallery, London/Superstock